WRESTLING

MADNESS

A Ringside Look at Wrestling Superstars

Matt Hunter

SMITHMARK

SMITHMARK books are available for bulk purchase for sales promotion and premium use. For details, write or call the manager of special sales, SMITHMARK Publishers, 115 West 18th Street, New York, NY 10011; 212-519-1215

Produced by SMITHMARK PUBLISHERS
115 West 18th Street, New York, NY 10011.

All trademarks used within are the property of their respective owners. SMITHMARK Publishers makes no claim to any trademarks other than their own.

Creative Direction: Kristen Schilo, Gato & Maui Productions
Art Direction: Jay Anning, Thumb Print
Graphic Design: Stephanie H. Pine

Library of Congress Cataloging-in-Publication Data

Hunter, Matt.
      Wrestling Madness : a ringside look at wrestling superstars / Matt Hunter.
          p.   cm.
      ISBN 0-7651-1740-1 hardcover
      1. Wrestlers Biography. 2. Wrestling-History. I. Title.
      GV1196.A1H86   1999
      796.812'092273—dc21
      [B]   99-23859

CIP

Printed and bound in Hong Kong

10 9 8 7 6 5 4 3 2 1

Photo Credits

Below (left to right): John Barrett, Duane C. Long (Sabu), Jeff Eisenberg, Steve Beyer, Russell C. Turiak, Howard Kernats; CORBIS/Bettmann, Duane C. Long, Ray Amati (Lou Albano), CORBIS/Wally McNamee, Howard Kernats, and Duane C. Long.

Introduction: *Wrestling: As You Like It* was published weekly by Wayli, Inc.

AP/Wide World Photos: p.15

Ray Amati: p.14

John Barrett: p.19 (all three), 20, 23, 27, 48, 49, 53 (right), 62 (right)

Steve Beyer: p.10, 33 (left and right), 39, 50, 57

Marc Breault: p.28, 38, 46, 51, 52, 53 (left)

Blackjack Brown: p.40 (right), 47

Corbis/Allen Brisson-Smith: p.61

Corbis/Marko Cuff: p.43

Corbis/Bettmann: p.8

Corbis/Mike Brennan: p.9, 62

Corbis/Wally McNamee: p.36

Corbis/Marko Shark: p.34

Corbis/Mark Solomon: p.60

Jeff Eisenberg: p.42

Howard Kernats: p.21, 22 (right), 24–25, 30, 40 (left), 41, 55 (left), 58

Duane C. Long: p.13, 16, 26, 29, 44 (left)

Reuters/Joe Skipper/Archive Photos: p. 63 (left)

Pro Wrestling Illustrated: Title page

Pro Wrestling Illustrated/Bill Apter: p.31

Pro Wrestling Illustrated/Frank Vitucci: p.54

Russell C. Turiak: p.11, 20 (inset), 22 (left), 23 (inset), 32, 35, 37, 39 (left), 56

Timothy Walker: p.17, 44 (right), 45, 55 (right), 59 (left and right)

UPI/Corbis/Bettmann: p.18 (left and right)

A special thank you to Stephen Ciacciarelli at Wrestling World

Contents

Introduction 4

Gorgeous George 8

Jerry Lawler 10

Mil Mascaras 12

Capt. Lou Albano 14

Abdullah the Butcher 16

Andre the Giant 18

"Stone Cold" Steve Austin 20

Bam Bam Bigelow 22

The Dudleys 24

"Nature Boy" Ric Flair 26

Mick Foley 28

Bill Goldberg 30

Scott Hall 32

Bret "The Hitman" Hart 34

"Hollywood" Hogan 36

Kevin Nash 38

"Diamond" Dallas Page 40

Sable 42

Sabu 44

Perry Saturn 46

"Macho Man" Randy Savage 48

Scott Steiner 50

Sting 52

Taz 54

The Undertaker 56

Rob Van Dam 58

Governor Jesse Ventura 60

Celebrity Madness 62

Wrestling Chronology 64

Introduction

To ask the question "When did wrestling begin?" is not unlike asking the question, "When did eating begin?" or "When did time begin?" It's impossible to know for certain, but the odds are good that as long as there have been living creatures on the planet, there has been wrestling. Look at a pair of young puppies roughhousing in the dirt; that's a form of wrestling. Consider a pair of bull moose locking antlers in a territorial battle for supremacy; that's a form of wrestling, too.

Tag team wrestling was first introduced in the United States in 1901 in San Francisco.

The earliest men no doubt fought each other for the best part of the cave, the most desirable mate, and the tastiest morsels of food. These, then, were the first forms of wrestling.

If you strip away all the excess baggage that wrestling has acquired over the years—eliminate the outfits and the foreign objects, the theme music and the fireworks, the cages, the barbed-wire, and the baseball bats—you'll see that wrestling is, in fact, the purest form of sport there is. One man's physical abilities are matched against another man's physical abilities, with nothing but pure wits, cunning, determination, and stamina determining the outcome.

There are references in the Bible to wrestling. In Genesis, Chapter 32, Verses 24 and 25, for example, the text reads: "So Jacob was left alone, and a man wrestled with him till daybreak. When the man saw that he could not overpower him, he touched the socket of Jacob's hip so that his hip was wrenched as he wrestled with the man."

In ancient China and Egypt, wrestling as a sport began to be developed. In ancient Greece, wrestling was part of a soldier's training and every young man's education, and it is not uncommon to find Greek sculpture, murals, and vases bearing images of two men wrestling. Greek literature writes of wrestling being the sport of gods and kings as well as of soldiers and common men. The Greeks understood that physical grace amidst fierce physical battle was an important quality to have, and placed a high premium on the one-on-one athletic competition that wrestling provided. The eighteenth ancient Olympic Games, held in 704 B.C., included wrestling.

On January 26, 1934, New York State passed a law banning the use of the dropkick in wrestling matches.

To win an ancient wrestling match, an athlete needed to throw his opponent to the ground three times so that he landed on his hip, shoulder, or back. As in the modern version of the sport, biting was not allowed. Attacking one's opponent by breaking his fingers, however, was permissible.

Mural painting in a tomb near Beni Hasan. Dynasty XII about 1900 B.C.

Ironically, some of the same problems that would haunt wrestling in the twentieth century haunted wrestling in the seventh century B.C.: Allegations of bribery and fixed matches affected the widespread appeal of the sport, which would remain relatively dormant for many centuries to follow.

Wrestling in the United States first began to enjoy popularity in the late 1800s, following a surge of popularity in England and Scotland. In 1880, William Muldoon became the first famous wrestling champion, battling for $10 purses in wrestling bouts ($7 went to the winner, $3 to the loser). By the early 1900s, both wrestling and boxing were popular sports in the United States, with early wrestling champions of the century including George Hackenschmidt (1904), Frank Gotch (1908), Ed "Strangler" Lewis (1920), Stanislaus Zbyszko (1925), and Gus Sonnenberg (1929).

In April 1957, legendary wrestler Danny Hodge appeared on the cover of *Sports Illustrated*.

Wrestlers, third century, B.C.

In April 1945, baseball legend Babe Ruth served as a special referee for wrestling matches in Maine and Massachusetts.

French poster of wrestlers circa 1899.

The twentieth century's first real explosion of interest in pro wrestling came in the 1950s. The reason: television. Here was a brand-new medium hungry for programming, and wrestling was only too happy to oblige. Families would huddle around their sets for the Friday-night or Saturday-night bouts to watch a weekly ritual of sanctioned violence. Television also produced wrestling's first true superstar: Gorgeous George (see page 8).

Interestingly, the century's second explosion of interest in pro wrestling, which took place in the 1980s, coincided with another technological innovation: cable television. Again, there was a huge need for sports programming, and wrestling was there to fill the void.

As the century draws to a close, the sport is undergoing yet another resurgence of popularity. This time, the primary driver isn't technology but attitude. No longer does the sport rely on standard good guy vs. bad guy themes to draw the audiences' attention. The end of the millennium has meant the rise of the antihero in wrestling. Popularity isn't necessarily connected to doing the right thing; instead, it's connected to winning at all costs. The sport has entered an era in which the end justifies the means.

So someone like Steve Austin, who openly flaunts his disdain for rules and authority, is massively popular. Someone like Sable, whose surgical enhancements won her the cover of *Playboy* magazine, hears enormous cheers. Even "Hollywood" Hogan, who once exhorted fans to say their prayers and take their vitamins, has since told the fans to "stick it"—and, as a result, has become more popular than ever.

On the pages that follow, you'll see photos and profiles of these stars and more . . . all part of the sports phenomenon that can only be called . . . WRESTLING MADNESS!

Wrestling's first sleeperhold was applied on June 29, 1931, by Jim Londos in a match against Ray Steele in New York's Yankee Stadium.

Wrestling's first masked wrestler debuted in Paris in 1873. He was known simply as "The Masked Wrestler."

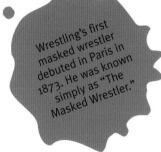

Books and magazines on pro wrestling, like these classics from the 1950s, have always been as popular as the sport itself.

Gorgeous George

He was the first wrestling superstar of the modern era, not the best of athletes but a master of psychological warfare, and a true product of the television era.

"Gorgeous" George Wagner was the man everybody loved to hate. In a sport filled with cigar-chomping brawlers and street-tough scrappers, Gorgeous George was utterly outrageous, with his bleached-blond hair and his demands that the ring—and his opponents!—be sprayed with perfume before he would even *think* of climbing through the ropes.

Born in Seward, Nebraska, George Wagner began his pro wrestling career when he was about fourteen years old, but it wasn't until he was around twenty-four that he developed the persona that would make him famous as the "Toast of the Coast," the "Sensation of the Nation," and "The Human Orchid."

At a time when no "real man" would be caught dead wearing anything remotely frilly, Gorgeous George paid approximately $1,000 apiece for the frilliest and fanciest of robes. Of course, George wouldn't put the robe on himself; no, that task was left to one of his valets, Geoffrey or Thomas Ross.

George also pioneered the use of entrance music, strutting to the ring to the sounds of "Pomp And Circumstance," the same music used by "Macho Man" Randy Savage. All this ballyhoo added up to a persona that was both infuriating and fascinating. Fans hated him, but they couldn't get enough of him. When Gorgeous George was on the card, attendance was sure to skyrocket.

In 1949, Gorgeous George starred in the movie *Alias The Champ,* but it was as a television star that he made his biggest mark. The new medium was hungry for new personalities, and the television camera loved George as much as he loved television. It's been said that aside from Milton Berle, Gorgeous George was responsible for selling more television sets in the early days of TV than anyone else.

His out-of-the-ring life was as flamboyant as his ring persona. His personal fortune was made, lost, and remade several times, and he married and divorced twice. On November 7, 1962, the wrestling world was stunned when George bet his hair against the mask of The Destroyer. George lost the match—and was shaved bald!

Gorgeous George died the day after Christmas in 1963, the result of a heart attack in his Hollywood apartment. Though he was only forty-eight, his impact on the sport was immeasurable. He was the first real entertainer in a sport that has since become known as "sports entertainment."

He was, in all respects, one of a kind.

Fastidious and precise about his appearance, Gorgeous George was also a fan of boxing, the other great ring sport.

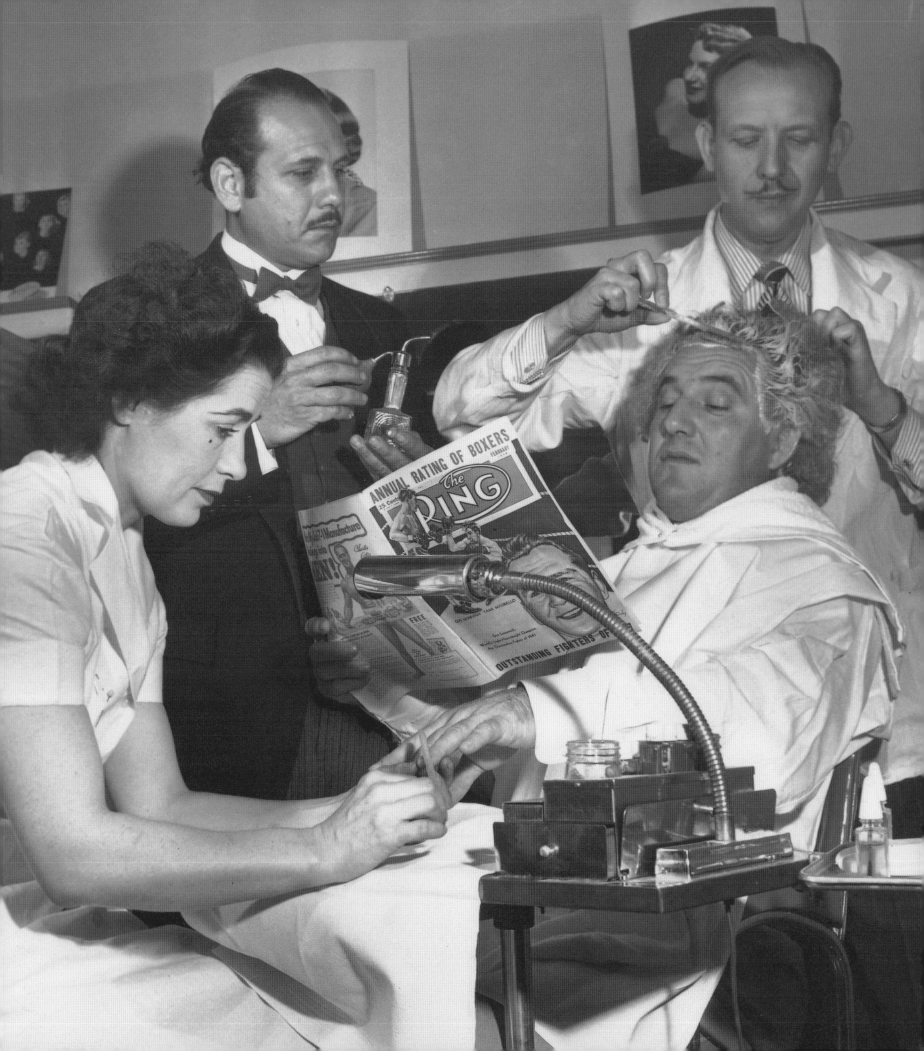

Jerry "The King" Lawler

Don't tell Jerry Lawler he isn't "The King."

This man owns Memphis the way Elvis Presley himself never even did: Lawler, not Presley, holds the records for arena attendance in Memphis. Lawler, not any other wrestler, has held the Mid-Southern heavyweight title more times than anyone else alive. Lawler, not anyone else, will go down in wrestling history as, by far, the greatest wrestler Memphis has ever produced.

Ironic, then, that his legacy to the sport may well be that he faced off against not a wrestler, but a well-known comedian.

In 1979, Andy Kaufman was a top television star, playing Latka Gravas on the comedy series "Taxi." He also began "wrestling" women as part of his offbeat nightclub act. He declared himself "Intergender Champion" and flaunted his non-existent athletic ability every chance he got by offering $1,000 to any woman who could pin his shoulders to the mat. In 1981, Kaufman was featured on the undercard of a wrestling event at Cobo Arena in Detroit, and in October of that year "defended" his "title" against a *Playboy* Playmate in Atlantic City, New Jersey.

On October 12, 1981, Kaufman appeared in Lawler's backyard, "wrestling" three women at the Mid-South Coliseum in Memphis. He defeated two, and wrestled to a draw with a third; they had a rematch on November 23, 1981.

Lawler had enough of these shenanigans. On April 5, 1982, Lawler and Kaufman squared off in the ring. "The King" delivered two piledrivers that sent Kaufman to the hospital for three days and captured headlines around the world. Kaufman emerged from the hospital wearing a neck brace.

On July 28, 1982, Kaufman and Lawler appeared on "Late Night With David Letterman." The animosity between the two was clearly never higher, as they engaged in a profanity-laden shouting match that had Letterman stunned, and ultimately ended with Kaufman throwing Letterman's coffee in Lawler's face before storming off the set. The incident made front page headlines nationwide.

In a fascinating footnote: History repeated itself somewhat in 1998 as Lawler wound up giving actor Jim Carrey a minor neck injury during the filming of the movie *Man On The Moon*—a biography of Andy Kaufman.

Meanwhile, Lawler continues to entertain and outrage as a commentator on World Wrestling Federation broadcasts. The career of "The King" is far from over—long live "The King!"

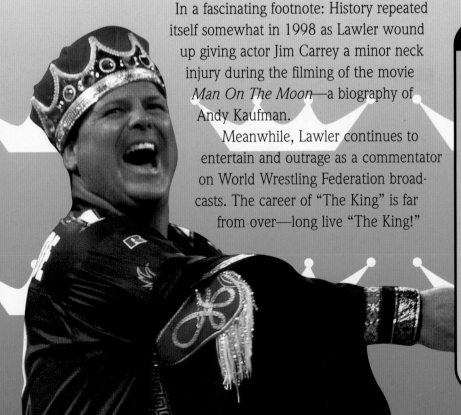

VITAL STATS

HEIGHT/WEIGHT
6', 234 lbs.

BIRTH DATE
November 29, 1949

PRO DEBUT
1970

CHAMPIONSHIP GOLD
One AWA World heavyweight title.

WATCH OUT FOR
Lawler's commentary on WWF broadcasts. He is both hilarious and offensive, often in the same sentence, but he is never dull.

MAXIMUM MADNESS
As the top star in the red-hot Memphis area in the '70s and '80s, Lawler wrestled—and defeated!—just about every top star in the sport, including Hulk Hogan, Ric Flair, Randy Savage, and Harley Race!

Jerry "The King" Lawler has secured his place in wrestling history, both in the wrestling ring as well as in the broadcaster's booth.

Mil Mascaras

In a sport in which every competitor is something of a special attraction, it takes a truly unique quality to stand out above the rest. Andre the Giant did it with size. Abdullah the Butcher did it with brutality. Mil Mascaras did it with consummate sportsmanship and a ring style that combined spectacular athleticism with gentlemanly grace.

Like millions of other Mexican children, Aaron Rodriguez (aka Mil Mascaras) grew up idolizing masked wrestling legend El Santo the way American kids in the '40s grew up idolizing John Wayne. So when Aaron took the name Mil Mascaras and entered the sport at the age of twenty-two, he was determined to use his hero as a model. Few would dispute that Mascaras matched—if not surpassed—El Santo's legendary reputation for athleticism and fair play.

Mascaras was like a painting come to life! His physique was as perfect as any man's could possibly be. His powerful upper body was complemented by incredibly strong legs. His conditioning was legendary. His knowledge of the pure science of wrestling holds and maneuvers was said to be second to none. His aerial skills were a thing of beauty. His outfits were impeccable. His amazing matches left fans and opponents alike breathless.

And the masks! Mascaras would come bounding into the ring all muscle and color, his eye-catching cape flowing in the air. As the fans cheered, he would flamboyantly remove his cape, then move to the center of the ring to hear the referee's instructions. Returning to his corner to prepare for the match, he would remove his mask to reveal—another, usually flashier, mask! Not surprisingly, the name "Mil Mascaras" means "man of a thousand masks." His collection, though, surely numbered several thousand.

When the match was underway, no matter how dastardly his foe's tactics, Mascaras was ever the supreme sportsman. It has been said that over the course of any given year, the number of rules Mascaras broke in all of his matches combined could be counted on one hand . . . and it would be more than likely that there would be several fingers left over.

In all that he did, Mascaras was the personification of sophistication and grace. It showed in the ring, and the fans embraced him worldwide, making him a superstar not only in his native Mexico, but also in the United States, Japan, and anywhere else he wrestled.

The man of a thousand masks was truly one in a million!

Mil Mascaras, whose name means "man of a thousand masks," is acknowledged by most experts as the best masked wrestler of all time.

VITAL STATS

HEIGHT/WEIGHT
5'11", 245 lbs.

BIRTH DATE
July 15, 1942

PRO DEBUT
1964

CHAMPIONSHIP GOLD
A wide range of regional titles throughout the United States and Mexico.

WATCH OUT FOR
The flying bodypress from the top rope. Nobody before or since has executed the move with such picturesque grace or decisive effectiveness.

MAXIMUM MADNESS
Mil Mascaras is one of Mexico's all-time top box office attractions —he's made more than thirty action movies!

Capt. Lou Albano

He was known as, quite simply, "The Manager Of Champions." And rightly so. Because when it came to managing tag teams to WWF World tag team championships, nobody did it better than The Captain. Want evidence?

Well, here's some: In 1980 Albano guided The Samoans to not one, but two reigns as WWF tag team champions. A year later, he led The Moondogs to the belts. When they lost the title, he regained the gold with Mr. Fuji and Mr. Saito, who captured the belts again in 1982. In 1983, The Samoans came back to win the belts once again.

And so on . . . and so on . . . and so on . . . .

When you tally up all the numbers, Albano led fourteen different duos to eighteen different WWF World tag team championships! Prior to his 1987 retirement, Capt. Lou was the ultimate personification of tag team wrestling.

A large part of his success was undoubtedly the empathy he felt with his charges. If he was managing The Moondogs, he'd come to the ring wearing tattered jeans, just like his men. If he was managing Fuji and Saito, the Japanese flag adorned his headband. Samoans? There was Albano in his Hawaiian shirt!

Albano came to managing as a wrestler. He was a member of The Sicilians with Tony Altimore, a moderately successful tag team that captured the WWF International tag team title in 1967. But his skills as a wrestler were nothing special. As a tactician, however, he was superb, and he proved it by guiding The Mongols to the WWF International tag team title in 1970.

Following his success as a rulebreaking manager, through the early part of the '80s, The Captain saw the light, changed his rulebreaking ways, and became a fan favorite. His popularity soared. In 1985, he appeared in Cyndi Lauper's megahit video, "Girls Just Wanna Have Fun." In 1986, he recorded an album with critically acclaimed musicians NRBQ, entitled "Lou & The Q," and snagged a featured role in the movie *Wise Guys*. Video game fans might recall the "Super Mario Bros. Super Show!" that debuted in 1989—yes, that was none other than Capt. Lou starring as Mario!

Now retired from the sport for good, the colorful and fast-talking Albano has left behind a legacy of excellence that is second to none . . . and a record of championships that won't soon be broken!

VITAL STATS

HEIGHT/WEIGHT
5'9", 227 lbs.

BIRTH DATE
July 29, 1933

PRO DEBUT
1953 (as a wrestler)
1969 (as a manager)

CHAMPIONSHIP GOLD
Two WWF International tag team titles (as a wrestler), eighteen WWF World tag team titles (as a manager).

WATCH OUT FOR
A comeback! The Captain could, at any time, lend his expertise to any tag team in the world. The result would undoubtedly be instant success!

MAXIMUM MADNESS
In December 1984, Roddy Piper attacked Lou Albano at an awards ceremony in New York's Madison Square Garden. Cyndi Lauper, a friend of Albano's, was also a victim. The result? WrestleMania I and the rock 'n' wrestling connection!

Always colorful, always entertaining, and never at a loss for something to say, Capt. Lou Albano is one of the greatest managers the sport has ever known.

Abdullah the Butcher

Abdullah the Butcher is aptly named. He's not a wrestler. He's not an athlete. That he found a home in professional wrestling is probably a sheer whim of fate.

"Butcher" is appropriate, for Abdullah is a bloodthirsty creature of pure violence who exists to wreak pure havoc. This native of the Sudan doesn't care much for rules, and his ring strategy can best be described in one word: maim.

A typical Abdullah match goes something like this: The bell rings, and Abdullah gets an animalistic gleam of impending pleasure in his eyes. His unfortunate opponent tries to mount a typical wrestling attack, but there's no defense for Abdullah's lust for violence. The Butcher grabs his opponent's head and begins gnawing on the soft flesh between the eyes. Blood begins to flow, which only feeds Abdullah's hunger for more, so he utilizes a sharp fork that he's had hidden in his trunks to inflict even more damage. The Butcher throws his foe to the canvas and astonishingly hurls his 360 bulky pounds into the air to deliver a thunderous elbowsmash that takes all the air and fight out of his foe.

A bit more bleeding, a bit more violence, a terrified referee's three-count, and Abdullah has scored yet another ugly and messy victory.

Incredible to think that he's been unleashing such violence since 1958—eight years before Bill Goldberg was even born!

While he's never won a world title, Abdullah the Butcher isn't a competitor for whom championship gold has been very important (though he has won a wide range of smaller regional championships in North America, as well as titles in Puerto Rico and Japan). For the Butcher, winning isn't all that important. Frighteningly enough, Abdullah's career has always been about inflicting pain and suffering, pure and simple, and the bloodier the better.

Abdullah may not be very graceful or athletic, but when it comes to violence, the Butcher has it down to a science.

Abdullah carves up the flesh on the head of Terry Funk during another typical Butcher bloodbath.

VITAL STATS

HEIGHT/WEIGHT
6'1", 360 lbs.

BIRTH DATE
January 16, 1941

PRO DEBUT
1958

CHAMPIONSHIP GOLD
Several regional titles in Puerto Rico, Japan, and North America.

WATCH OUT FOR
The foreign object. Abdullah is a master at utilizing forks, knives, and all manner of deadly weapons hidden in his ample waistband.

MAXIMUM MADNESS
Abdullah the Butcher trains for his violent matches by eating chicken . . . raw . . . with the feathers still attached!

Andre the Giant

Andre Rene Roussimoff was born in Grenoble, France. Both his parents were more than six feet tall, as are his four siblings; his grandfather was a giant, too, standing 7'8" tall.

When Andre was seventeen years old, he worked moving furniture in Paris. He was discovered by some wrestlers while training in a gym, and the result was the start of a career that would make him one of the most recognized celebrities in the world.

Andre's career wasn't about winning championships, though. His designation as "The People's Champion" was the only title he ever really needed. It was about winning fans and, not incidentally, battle royals. Andre was legendary for his battle royal prowess, and first became a worldwide celebrity in the sport by winning multiple battle royals in the Los Angeles area in the '70s.

Andre's size and celebrity made him a special attraction wherever he went. Promoters worldwide scrambled for his services. When a big card was taking place, it wasn't truly big unless Andre was on the bill. On June 25, 1976, for example, when fans in New York's Shea Stadium watched boxer Muhammad Ali battle wrestler Antonio Inoki on TV from Tokyo, they saw Andre battle boxer Chuck Wepner in person. *Sports Illustrated* ran a major profile on him in its December 21, 1981, issue; it was, up to that point (and appropriately) the largest profile they had run on any single athlete.

It wasn't long before Hollywood came calling, and Andre won roles in the popular television series "Six Million Dollar Man" (1974) and "The Fall Guy" (1981). He appeared in bit parts in the films *Conan the Destroyer* (1984) and *Micki + Maude* (1984) before landing the critically acclaimed role as Fezzik in *The Princess Bride* (1987).

Sadly, the man known worldwide as "The Gentle Giant" turned brutal during the last years of his career. He feuded with Hulk Hogan, who was massively popular at the time. Their war culminated in a spectacular main event bout at WrestleMania III on March 29, 1987; the event drew 93,173 people to the Pontiac Silverdome, saw Hogan retain his WWF World title, and to this day remains North America's highest all-time live attendance record for pro wrestling.

VITAL STATS

HEIGHT/WEIGHT
7'4", 520 lbs.

BIRTH DATE
May 19, 1946

PRO DEBUT
1964

CHAMPIONSHIP GOLD
One WWF World tag team title.

WATCH OUT FOR
The size-22 foot to the face, followed by Andre literally sitting on his opponent to score the win. Owtch!

MAXIMUM MADNESS
A prodigious beer-drinker, Andre would frequently drink two cases of beer per day—and once consumed 117 bottles of beer in one sitting!

Andre died of a heart attack in January 1993, but the legend of Andre the Giant continues to grow ever larger. Stickers, decals, and street art bearing Andre's likeness have become one of the most frequently seen bits of urban graffiti worldwide. It's a phenomenon that Andre—hero or villain—would have appreciated.

Whether intimidating wrestlers like Randy Savage and Hulk Hogan, or threatening managers like Bobby "The Brain" Heenan, Andre was an overpowering presence in the ring.

At the peak of his fame, Andre the Giant was, literally and figuratively, the biggest celebrity in the sporting world, approaching Muhammad Ali in recognition.

"Stone Cold" Steve Austin

VITAL STATS

HEIGHT/WEIGHT
6'2", 252 lbs.

BIRTH DATE
December 18, 1964

PRO DEBUT
1989

CHAMPIONSHIP GOLD
One WCW U.S. title; one WCW World tag team title; three WWF World tag team titles; two WWF Intercontinental titles; two WWF World heavyweight titles.

WATCH OUT FOR
A hard whip into the ropes, followed by the feared "Stone Cold" stunner, one of the most effective finishing moves in wrestling.

MAXIMUM MADNESS
In the fall of 1995, he was fired by WCW, and then was defeated by Mikey Whipwreck in ECW, but at the 1996 King of the Ring tournament, Austin beat Jake Roberts in the finals to become the WWF's "King."

"Stone Cold" Steve Austin is undoubtedly one of the top wrestlers in the world. How do we know?

Because "Stone Cold" said so . . . and that's the bottom line!

When "Stone Cold" Steve Austin won the WWF World title from Shawn Michaels at WrestleMania XIII on March 24, 1997, it started one of the most watched and most sensational chapters in wrestling history: the feud between Austin and WWF boss Vince McMahon Jr.

McMahon didn't think Austin was the WWF's type of champion. McMahon wanted a champion who would tell the fans to work out, say their prayers, and take their vitamins. Austin, who cursed and chugged beer, certainly wasn't that type, so McMahon set out to destroy him. Thanks to the feud between the boss and Austin, the WWF's Monday-night "Raw is War" broadcast is the most-watched show on cable TV.

Steve Austin, superstar? That didn't seem likely in 1995, when Austin was told by World Championship Wrestling (WCW) President Eric Bischoff that his services were no longer needed. Back on August 18, 1994, Austin lost the WCW U.S. title to Hacksaw Duggan, and shortly afterward he suffered a detached tricep while wrestling in Japan. The injuries piled up, and in late 1995, WCW officials decided they had lost patience with the battered thirty-year-old who wore simple black trunks in the ring.

Then came the turning point in Austin's career. Shortly after signing with the WWF, he won the 1996 King of the Ring tournament. He started calling himself "Stone Cold" and adopted the slogan that would make him famous: "Austin 3:16." On August 3, 1997, Austin beat Owen Hart for his first WWF Intercontinental title, but almost had his career ended by Hart's piledriver. It was simply through pure courage that Austin was able to crawl over to Hart and cover him for the pin. But the piledriver had severely damaged his neck and doctors said his career could be over.

Austin refused to give up, and McMahon's refusal to let him back into the ring without medical approval ignited the feud that has fascinated the wrestling world ever since. Austin has inflicted several severe batterings on McMahon, who has fought back by buying off wrestlers to destroy "Stone Cold."

Although Austin has held up well in his feud with McMahon, he lost the title on September 27, 1998, and had trouble getting it back through '98. But his popularity continues to soar . . . and that's the bottom line!

"Stone Cold" Steve Austin is the most popular wrestler in the sport today. Back in 1995, though, nobody would have imagined that Austin would be the man to lead the WWF into the twenty-first century.

Bam Bam Bigelow

He used to be a professional bounty hunter. If that doesn't tell you just about all you need to know about Bam Bam Bigelow, read on.

His bald head is crowned by colorful tattoos of flames, and he is considered one of the toughest and strongest men in the world. Yet, despite his imposing presence and undeniable skill, Bigelow has never won a WWF or WCW World, U.S., or Intercontinental title, and is considered by many wrestling experts to be an underachiever.

In late 1998, Bigelow invaded WCW and had no trouble getting the attention of then-World champion Bill Goldberg. He attacked Goldberg in the locker room area and demanded a title match. Although Goldberg fended off Bigelow's challenge, many credit Bigelow with creating the distraction that broke Goldberg's famed concentration and eventually led to him losing the belt to Kevin Nash.

Bigelow was one of the first graduates of The Monster Factory, a training school for wrestlers in southern New Jersey. He made an immediate impact when he entered the sport in 1985—he won the World Class Championship Wrestling TV title, and even appeared in *Sports Illustrated.*

Bigelow is a nomad. He refuses to stay in one federation for a long period of time, and has spent time in the WWF, WCW, Extreme Championship Wrestling (ECW), most major independents, and Japan. If one charted Bigelow's illustrious career, the years would follow a jagged line of ups and downs, with very few periods of stability.

Despite his ferocity and intimidating presence, Bigelow's most famous match resulted in an embarrassing defeat. At WrestleMania XI on April 2, 1995, he was pinned by former NFL star Lawrence Taylor in 11 minutes, 42 seconds.

Bigelow is one of the few independent free agents left in wrestling, so it's not surprising he has done his best work in the independent federations. Bigelow, Chris Candido, and Shane Douglas, known as The Triple Threat, were an outstanding trio in ECW for nearly two years before Bigelow departed for WCW in late 1998. Yet there was upheaval in The Triple Threat when Bigelow defeated Shane Douglas for the ECW heavyweight title on October 16, 1997. Bigelow briefly left the Threat, but returned in early 1998 after losing the belt to Douglas. On March 1, 1998, Bigelow ended one of wrestling's longest winning streaks when he pinned Taz for the ECW TV title.

Perhaps it's unreasonable to expect Bigelow to ever settle down in a federation for a long time and win a world title. But it's more than reasonable to expect that fans are in for a great match when they hear the loud cries of "Bam! Bam!"

Bam Bam Bigelow's head is tattooed with flames, which helps make him as visually imposing as he is physically intimidating. A woman like Luna (opposite page), though, isn't intimidated by Bigelow; she has her own unique and intimidating look.

VITAL STATS

HEIGHT/WEIGHT
6'3", 368 lbs.

BIRTH DATE
September 1, 1961

PRO DEBUT
1985

CHAMPIONSHIP GOLD
One ECW heavyweight title; one ECW TV title.

WATCH OUT FOR
The big man climbing the ropes. Although Bigelow's huge, he's also agile, and capable of executing a graceful and powerful dive from above.

MAXIMUM MADNESS
Bigelow and Shane Douglas were feuding in 1997 and were set to face each other in a tag team match at ECW Arena. But Bigelow attacked his partner, Taz, and gave the three-finger Triple Threat salute.

The Dudleys

Sign Guy Dudley. Spike Dudley. "Big" Dick Dudley. Sometimes, it seems there's a new Dudley appearing every week in ECW, but the Dudleys that everyone's paying attention to—and opponents are watching out for—are D-Von and Buh-Buh Ray, the five-time ECW tag team champions and self-proclaimed most dangerous tag team in the world. It's hard to argue with them. In fact, it's downright *foolish* to argue with them!

Fact: The Dudleys will challenge anyone.

Fact: The Dudleys will accept challenges from anyone.

Fact: When The Dudleys beat Masato Tanaka and Balls Mahoney on November 6, 1998, for their fifth ECW tag team crown, they became ECW's most successful team ever. Although the Dudleys lost the belts to Rob Van Dam and Sabu, their achievement is etched forever in the pages of wrestling history.

And history shows that the Dudleys are one team that can't be denied.

D-Von and Buh-Buh Ray won their first ECW tag team title when they defeated The Eliminators on April 13, 1997, at ECW Arena in Philadelphia. This was an important victory for the Dudleys because, at the time, The Eliminators were considered the top tag team in ECW.

That first title reign lasted less than a month before the Dudleys lost the belts to The Eliminators, but they bounced right back to beat The Eliminators for the second time on June 20, 1997, in Waltham, Massachusetts. That title reign also lasted less than a month. Their third championship, which began when they beat The Gangstas on August 17, 1997, broke the thirty-day barrier, but just barely. Their fourth title reign lasted only eight days. Their fifth title reign lasted only thirty-eight days.

Despite their brief reigns, The Dudleys have made their mark on ECW. Maybe they'll win five more tag titles. Maybe each reign will last less than a week. But they've beaten the best, and they'll never back down from anyone.

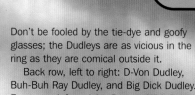

Don't be fooled by the tie-dye and goofy glasses; the Dudleys are as vicious in the ring as they are comical outside it.
Back row, left to right: D-Von Dudley, Buh-Buh Ray Dudley, and Big Dick Dudley. Front row, left to right: Dances With Dudley, Sign Guy Dudley, and Chubby Dudley.

"Nature Boy" Ric Flair

"The Man." "Nature Boy." "Slick Ric."

How about Mr. Miracle?

Or *something*, because it's time to come up with a new nickname for the man born Richard Fliehr, who was raised in Minnesota, and who has become indelibly etched in the annals of wrestling history.

It's incredible to think he almost didn't make it.

On October 4, 1975, less than three years into Flair's pro career, the Cessna 310 plane he was on crashed in North Carolina. He suffered a broken back. Then, on May 24, 1976, less than eight months after doctors said he'd never wrestle again, he captured his second Mid-Atlantic heavyweight title, defeating Wahoo McDaniel.

Since then, Flair has collected championships like nobody before or since. In doing so, he's also established an undeniable position as not only one of the best wrestlers of the '80s or the '90s, or even the latter half of the twentieth century, but also as one of the greatest wrestlers of all time.

He's proven himself to be a superb scientific wrestler, an excellent aerial tactician, and a master of psychological warfare. In May 1986, he formed The Four Horsemen, the clique that set the standard for groups like the NWO, DeGeneration X, and dozens of others that have since come and gone.

He's wrestled the finest stars of the past three decades, and beaten most of them for titles. The best of those stars can, if they're lucky, claim they've taken Flair to a 30-minute draw . . . or a 45-minute draw . . . or a 60-minute draw . . . or, on rare occasions, even a 90-minute draw.

Flair just keeps going . . . and going . . . and going.

Amazingly, it seems as if he'll never stop! On March 14, 1999, Flair defeated "Hollywood" Hulk Hogan to capture his sixth WCW World heavyweight title. The match took place seventeen days after Flair's fiftieth birthday.

Mr. Miracle, indeed!

"Whooooo!"

The "Nature Boy" has been wrestling professionally for nearly thirty years—and is recognized around the globe as one of the greatest competitors of all time.

VITAL STATS

HEIGHT/WEIGHT
6'1", 243 lbs.

BIRTH DATE
February 25, 1949

PRO DEBUT
1972

CHAMPIONSHIP GOLD
Eleven NWA World heavyweight championships; six WCW World heavyweight championships; two WWF World heavyweight championships; six NWA/WCW U.S. heavyweight championships; two NWA World tag team titles.

WATCH OUT FOR
Flair's cry of, "Now we're goin' to school!"—which means his legendary figure-four leglock is just moments away!

MAXIMUM MADNESS
The largest audience ever to witness wrestling? On April 29, 1995, in North Korea, 190,000 people were in attendance. The main event? Japanese legend Antonio Inoki vs. "Nature Boy" Ric Flair.

Mick Foley

If you don't know him as Mick Foley, maybe you know him as Mankind. Or Cactus Jack. Or Dude Love.

Talk about a split personality!

For the first eight years of his career, he was a virtual unknown, toiling night after night for small federations in front of tiny crowds. Opponents knew him as a fearless madman who loved brawling throughout an arena. But most WWF and WCW fans had never heard of Mick Foley.

Fast forward to December 29, 1998. Mick Foley, wrestling as Mankind, stepped into the ring against WWF World champion Rocky Maivia and did what nobody ever expected him to do: He won the WWF World title. One month later, just two days after losing the belt to Maivia at the 1999 Royal Rumble, he won his second WWF World title.

Just a brawler? Just a crazy puncher and kicker who would never get anywhere? Hardly. Mick Foley is a two-time former WWF World champion, and not just any brawler can say that. These days, he's also a hero of the people as he joins Steve Austin in a war against Vince McMahon's corporate team.

His repertoire is admittedly limited. He kicks and punches and loves using foreign objects like tables and chairs. Because of his various personalities as Mankind, Cactus Jack, Dude Love, and Mick Foley, opponents never know what or whose offense they're going to get. But he has thrilled fans and terrorized opponents all over the world. One time, WWF wrestlers petitioned to have his "mandible claw" banned because they felt it was an illegal chokehold. Mick is still using it as his finisher.

Wrestling as Cactus Jack, his career was nearly ended in early 1993 when he was powerbombed on a cement floor by Big Van Vader. Despite suffering from amnesia, he returned to action the following fall, proving his incredible resiliency. Mick served notice that he wasn't just a brawling maniac in 1994, when he and Kevin Sullivan teamed to win the WCW World tag team title. They held the belts for over two months before losing them to Paul Orndorff and Paul Roma. Many fans scoffed when he came to the WWF in 1996, but he proved himself by facing, and almost beating, World champion Shawn Michaels.

These days, nobody knows which Mick Foley is going to show up on any night. A rulebreaker one week, a fan favorite the next, Foley is consistent only in that he's always unorthodox. He just might be the greatest brawler of all time.

Whether he appears in the ring as Cactus Jack, Mankind, Dude Love, or just plain ol' Mick Foley, he's sure to offer opponents one of the most brutal matches of their careers.

Bill Goldberg

Born in Tulsa, Oklahoma, Goldberg had hopes of an NFL career, and played with the Atlanta Falcons and the Carolina Panthers before enrolling in WCW's Power Plant pro wrestling training school in 1997.

He never could have imagined he'd affect the mat sport the way he did.

Fans weren't particularly impressed when William Scott Goldberg made his way to the ring on September 22, 1997, for his first pro match. "Big deal," many probably thought, "another muscle-bound newcomer. Like we haven't seen guys like him a million times before. Ho-hum."

Yeah, right!

Goldberg won that match, against Hugh Morris. Then he won another. And another. And another. And before long, people started to be impressed. Who was this power-house with the unbeaten record? Signs began appearing in arenas that asked the question, "Who's next?" The answer was simple: Whoever was Goldberg's next opponent for the evening, to be added to the growing heap of fallen bodies that constituted the most impressive winning streak the sport has ever seen.

Goldberg was 66–0 when he received a U.S. title shot against Raven. Wham! Bam! Thank you, Raven: 67–0 and a U.S. heavyweight championship belt.

Goldberg was 106–0 when he received a WCW World title shot against "Hollywood" Hogan. Wham! Bam! Thank you, "Hollywood": 107–0 and the WCW World heavyweight title.

It took the interference of Scott Hall and an electric cattle prod for Kevin Nash to end Goldberg's World title reign and blemish his won-lost record (at 173–1), on December 27, 1998. But Goldberg isn't about to let anything stop him on his relentless march to wrestling immortality, whether it's the combined forces of the New World Order or a surprise jolt of voltage from Hall or anyone else.

Truly, Goldberg is the first pro wrestling megastar of the twenty-first century. His career, barely begun, will be an awesome spectacle in the years to come!

VITAL STATS

HEIGHT/WEIGHT
6'3", 285 lbs.

BIRTH DATE
December 27, 1966

PRO DEBUT
1997

CHAMPIONSHIP GOLD
One WCW World heavyweight title; one WCW U.S. heavyweight title.

WATCH OUT FOR
The spear and the jackhammer, the stunningly powerful one-two combination that won Goldberg the longest rookie unbeaten streak in wrestling history!

MAXIMUM MADNESS
On February 19, 1999, WCW star Goldberg had the audacity to challenge "Stone Cold" Steve Austin on national television—on "The Tonight Show" with Jay Leno!

who's nex

Goldberg is 285 pounds of solid muscle and intimidation . . . and he's becoming even more dominant an athlete with every match.

Scott Hall

"Who did you come to see?"

When Scott Hall grabbed the ring microphone and asked that question, he expected one of two answers from WCW fans: "NWO!" or "WCW!" But the fans who said "WCW!" were routinely ignored by this brash, egotistical, and arrogant wrestler who, simply by acting cool, has become one of the top stars in wrestling.

The truth is, millions of fans came to see Scott Hall.

Hall isn't asking his trademark question anymore. In fact, he wasn't asking any questions for a long time when, shortly after winning the WCW U.S. title at SuperBrawl '99, he suffered a serious ankle injury. But the fans know, and Scott Hall knows, that he will be back . . . bigger, louder, and brasher than ever.

Somewhere along the line, Hall slicked back his hair, stuck a toothpick in his mouth, and decided, "I like this look." Wrestling fans agreed, because after undergoing his transformation from Scott Hall to Razor Ramon in mid-1992, Hall finally made his mark on the sport. Sure, he has since returned to his original name, the one he was born with in Miami, Florida, but it was a simple change of name and attitude that turned Hall into a star.

For years after Hall made his pro debut in 1984, fans wondered why a 6'8", 290-pounder with so much athletic ability couldn't make his mark in the ring. Sure, he won the AWA World tag team title with Curt Hennig in 1986, but not until he developed the "diamond death drop," which he learned from former manager "Diamond" Dallas Page and renamed the "Razor's edge," did his career move upward.

And it has soared! He came close to winning the WWF World title, and captured the vacant WWF Intercontinental title on September 23, 1993. He held the title for seven months before losing the belt to Diesel (Kevin Nash), who would become his best friend and tag team partner. Finally, on May 27, 1996, he reverted back to Scott Hall, invaded WCW, and joined with Nash to change wrestling forever with the formation of the New World Order.

Although Hall has failed to win the WCW World heavyweight title over the past three years, his presence in WCW is always obvious, even when he's not around. Fans and opponents know that, at any time, Hall might swagger back into the building.

And if you're not on his side, you're in a lot of trouble!

Scott Hall, formerly Razor Ramon in the WWF, is a cornerstone of the renegade NWO organization in the WCW.

VITAL STATS

HEIGHT/WEIGHT
6'8", 290 lbs.

BIRTH DATE
October 20, 1958

PRO DEBUT
1984

CHAMPIONSHIP GOLD
One AWA World tag team title; three WWF Intercontinental titles; one WCW U.S. title; four WCW World tag team titles.

WATCH OUT FOR
The cocky look that breaks out on Hall's face whenever he's about to execute his "Razor's edge" finisher. He knows it's coming . . . and now, so do you!

MAXIMUM MADNESS
He was an underachiever for most of his career, but Hall didn't underachieve when he stepped into the ring on September 27, 1993, and beat Rick Martel for the WWF Intercontinental title.

Bret "The Hitman" Hart

From the day he was born in Calgary, Alberta, Bret "The Hitman" Hart was destined to become a professional wrestler. His father is Stu Hart, a legendary wrestler in Canada, and Stu trained Bret in the basement of their home. But it wasn't until August 26, 1990, nearly fourteen years after he made his professional debut, that "The Hitman" proved he could make it on his own.

Just five months earlier, Bret and longtime tag team partner Jim Neidhart—The Hart Foundation—decided to split up. The team had won two WWF World tag team championships, but Bret thirsted for singles competition. He stepped into the ring against Curt Hennig at SummerSlam '91 and walked out with the Intercontinental title wrapped around his waist!

That incredible victory was only the beginning for "the best there is, the best there was, and the best there ever will be."

Hart lost the Intercontinental title to The Mountie on January 17, 1992, but regained it four months later at WrestleMania VIII with a victory over Roddy Piper. He held on to the belt for five more months before losing it to his brother-in-law, Davey Boy Smith, in a hotly contested match at SummerSlam '92.

After losing the belt, Hart decided to try for bigger and better things. He set his sights on the WWF World title and, on October 12, 1992, won his first World title from "Nature Boy" Ric Flair.

Hart went on to compile a remarkable record in the WWF. He won four more World titles, yet his time in the WWF came to a disappointing conclusion. In 1997, with the wrestling world changing around him, Bret turned his back on his American fans and became vehemently pro-Canadian. Despite the fans' boos, he won his final WWF World title on August 3, 1997. But, just three months later, having already signed a contract with the rival WCW, Bret lost the belt to Shawn Michaels in a controversial match.

Although he has won three WCW U.S. titles, Bret's bitterness toward the U.S. fans has not subsided. His career has also been slowed by injuries.

Even so, he may have no more to prove. Arguably he truly is the best there is, the best there was, and the best there ever will be.

"The best there is, the best there was, the best there'll ever be." Few would argue with that assessment of Bret Hart's skills.

VITAL STATS

HEIGHT/WEIGHT
5'11", 235 lbs.

BIRTH DATE
July 2, 1957

PRO DEBUT
1976

CHAMPIONSHIP GOLD
Two WWF World tag team titles; two WWF Intercontinental titles; five WWF World heavyweight titles; three WCW U.S. titles.

WATCH OUT FOR
A leg takedown, which is always followed by "The Hitman's" signature finishing maneuver, the "sharpshooter" leglock. Few have escaped it.

MAXIMUM MADNESS
Bret Hart was about to leave the WWF in late 1997. WWF head Vince McMahon wanted him to lose the belt on purpose. Hart refused. But at the 1997 Survivor Series, Hart got caught in Shawn Michaels's "sharpshooter," and the referee called for the bell, even though Hart never submitted.

"Hollywood" Hogan

"Lemme tell ya, brother, the way to live right is to say your prayers, take your vitamins, and train hard every day."

Sound familiar? It should . . . if you were a Hulk Hogan fan back in 1985. Those were the days of "Hulkamania" and the "Hulkster," who was by far the most popular athlete in the sport. Every big foot to an opponent's face, and every legdrop and three-count victory that followed, was met with the kinds of deafening cheers that usually accompany only the most dramatic of Super Bowl touchdowns or World Series grand slams. As a five-time World Wrestling Federation World champion, Hogan led the WWF—and the sport as a whole—to new heights of popularity and mainstream acceptance.

But on July 7, 1996, Hogan threw it all away. Having left the WWF for the rival WCW, Hogan wiped his feet on the fans' cheers and spit right in their dreams. He joined forces with WWF outcasts Scott Hall and Kevin Nash to form the NWO—the New World Order, which quickly became the most powerful rulebreaking clique pro wrestling has ever known.

Yes, *rulebreaking*!

Incredibly, Hogan turned his back on all that made him wealthy and famous beyond imagination. He didn't care. For him, it was a return to his youth, a trip back in time to 1980, when he first entered the WWF as a hated rulebreaker, battling such beloved favorites as Andre the Giant and then-WWF World champion Bob Backlund.

Just as incredibly, Hogan's turn to rulebreaking in the late-1990s has made him at least as influential a force in the sport as he was in the mid-1980s.

Imagine what wonders the twenty-first century "Hulkster" will unveil!

VITAL STATS

HEIGHT/WEIGHT
6'8", 275 lbs.

BIRTH DATE
August 11, 1953

PRO DEBUT
1978

CHAMPIONSHIP GOLD
Five WWF World heavyweight titles; four WCW World heavyweight titles.

WATCH OUT FOR
The big boot to the face; that means the legdrop is next, followed by the inevitable three-count!

MAXIMUM MADNESS
On January 23, 1984, Hogan defeated The Iron Sheik in New York's Madison Square Garden to capture his first WWF World title and mark the official birth of "Hulkamania."

It was a dark day for wrestling when Hulk Hogan turned his back on the fans, joined the NWO, and reinvented himself as "Hollywood" Hogan.

Kevin Nash

It's hard to believe that Kevin Nash once charmed Kathy Lee Gifford and had WWF fans chanting his name. But those were in the days when Nash was known as Diesel, the hard-working fan favorite with the charming personality. Now known by his real name, Nash struts to the ring and refers to himself as "Big Sexy." And while "Hollywood" Hogan and Eric Bischoff get most of the attention, there's little doubt that Nash is the leader of the pack . . . the NWO Wolfpac, that is.

The New World Order has become wrestling's most feared, influential, and respected organization-within-an-organization, and it owes its genesis to Nash. In 1996, Nash left the WWF, where he had held the World heavyweight title for nearly a year, and teamed with Scott Hall, another former WWF star, to invade WCW. They called themselves The Outsiders. On June 16, 1996, Nash and Hall made wrestling history when they declared war on WCW.

Hulk Hogan joined the group shortly afterward, followed by Syxx, Ted DiBiase, Eric Bischoff, and The Giant. Today, after going through several changes—including one which saw the NWO split into two with Hall and Nash on opposite sides—a leaner, meaner NWO is still ruling the roost. Nash benefited from NWO interference to win his first WCW World title from Bill Goldberg at Starrcade '98. On January 4, 1999, Nash laid down and purposely lost the belt to Hogan.

A big-time powerful brawler who can throw in a few scientific moves, too, Nash has a right to walk with a swagger. Perhaps he even has a right to pull off his playful, though often dangerous, antics. He has, in only nine years, become one of the most famous wrestlers in the world. After a slow start with WCW in 1991 and 1992, he jumped to the WWF in 1993, changed his name to Diesel, and became Shawn Michaels' bodyguard.

But the bodyguard was more than that . . . he was a great wrestler! Within an eight-month period in 1994, Diesel won the WWF Inter-continental, World tag team, and World heavyweight titles, highlighted by a victory over Bob Backlund for the World title on November 26, 1994. His "jackknife" powerbomb became the sport's most lethal finishing maneuver.

Kevin Nash is a man who questions authority and refuses to play by the rules. Perhaps his career path isn't one to follow, but it's impossible to argue with his stellar results.

Kevin Nash, formerly known as Diesel in the WWF, has been a pivotal weapon in the war between WCW and the NWO.

VITAL STATS

HEIGHT/WEIGHT
7', 356 lbs.

BIRTH DATE
July 9, 1958

PRO DEBUT
1990

CHAMPIONSHIP GOLD
One WWF World heavyweight title; one WWF Intercontinental title; one WWF World tag team title; one WCW World heavyweight title; three WCW World tag team titles.

WATCH OUT FOR
A hard forearm or clothesline, which is almost always followed by the "jackknife" powerbomb, a move that shocks an opponent's body to the spine.

MAXIMUM MADNESS
Scott Hall promised he'd have some surprise guests when he invaded WCW in 1996. One of them turned out to be Kevin Nash, who left behind his "Diesel" moniker in the WWF and helped form the New World Order.

"Diamond" Dallas Page

Most professional wrestlers start their careers in the ring and, after retiring, consider becoming managers or broadcasters. But "Diamond" Dallas Page has never done things the conventional way. After all, this is a man who was once so down on his luck that he had to sell a pair of his wrestling tights to pay his bills.

Now that he's one of the most famous wrestlers in the world, it's hard to imagine that DDP—as he is called by his fans—started out back in 1988 as the manager of Badd Company, a tag team in the now-defunct AWA. Badd Company is long forgotten, but Dallas Page lives on as a wrestler . . . despite the best efforts of the NWO Wolfpac.

For most of the past four years, Page has fought a courageous, if seemingly futile, one-man battle against the NWO. The battle has endeared him to the fans, as he has sacrificed shots at championship gold for the good of the sport.

Page is an impressive wrestler. He packs 260 pounds of muscle on his well-toned body and is one of the more powerful men in WCW. His "diamond cutter" finisher is awesomely impressive, and he has held his own against extremely talented mat and aerial wrestlers alike.

But times weren't always so good for Page. After his stint as a manager in the AWA, he became a TV commentator for Florida Championship Wrestling. He returned to managing in the early 1990s before deciding a year later to become a full-time wrestler.

Although he won the WCW TV title in 1995, he was down on his luck soon afterward. His wife, Kimberly, joined with arch-rival Johnny B. Badd, and Page lost $6.6 million—every penny he had—to Kimberly when he was pinned by Badd on February 11, 1996.

Page left the sport. He was jobless. Finally, desperate for personal salvation, he returned to WCW as a fan favorite and started his climb to the top.

Page and Kimberly—who is now one of the Nitro Girls—reunited and were wrestling's most popular couple. He became even more popular when he turned down an offer to join the NWO. Despite the NWO's attempts to embarrass him, Page persevered. On December 28, 1997, he beat Curt Hennig for his first WCW U.S. title. On October 26, 1998, he won the U.S. belt from Bret Hart.

On April 11, 1999, DDP defeated Ric Flair, Hollywood Hogan, and Sting in a four-way dance at the Spring Stampede pay-per-view to capture the WCW World title. This rags-to-riches story isn't through being written yet!

"Diamond" Dallas Page has risen to the top of the sport through hard work, determination, and solid wrestling and brawling skills.

VITAL STATS

HEIGHT/WEIGHT
6'5", 260 lbs.

BIRTH DATE
April 5, 1949

PRO DEBUT
1991

CHAMPIONSHIP GOLD
Two WCW U.S. heavyweight titles; one WCW TV title; one WCW World heavyweight title.

WATCH OUT FOR
A fiercely rampaging Dallas Page, who has picked up the pace after his slow start and is setting up his opponent for the "diamond cutter" finisher.

MAXIMUM MADNESS
In 1996, Page was penniless and out of wrestling. He knew something had to change, so he changed himself. He took on a new attitude, became a fan favorite, and led the battle against the NWO.

Sable

Sable. One word says it all!

In a sport dominated by big, strong, violent men, a beautiful voluptuous blonde has become the most recognized personality of all. In her former life, she modeled for Guess jeans and Pepsi and shot a video for MTV. Now, as one of the most famous women in wrestling, she has appeared on the cover of *Playboy* magazine, *TV Guide,* and has fascinated millions of viewers. And no wonder. Sable is as gorgeous on the outside as she is tough on the inside. She has proven herself to be a no-nonsense woman who is perfectly capable of handling herself. At the 1998 Survivor Series, Sable pinned Jacquelyn for the WWF women's title!

Wrestling fans were first introduced to the sensational Sable at WrestleMania XII on March 31, 1996, when she accompanied Hunter Hearst Helmsley to the ring. After losing the match, Helmsley blamed Sable for the loss, and Marc Mero had to come to her rescue. The following night at the WWF's "Monday Night Raw" broadcast, Sable left the building in Mero's arms.

Little did Sable know that she had just transferred her allegiance from one egotistical male to another. When Mero won the Intercontinental title later that year, he couldn't stand the fact that the fans were more interested in Sable than himself. His jealousy grew and he increasingly treated her with disrespect.

Sable responded by becoming more aggressive. In January 1997, she had an in-ring argument with Mero that was seen by millions of television viewers. Meanwhile, Mero was becoming more jealous than ever, especially after Sable picked up two awards—Dressed to Kill and Miss Slammy—at the 1997 Slammy Awards.

The tension between Mero and Sable was put on hold as Sable engaged in a vicious feud with Luna Vachon, but their problems couldn't be put off forever. Shortly after Sable used Mero's finishing move, the TKO, to beat Luna at WrestleMania XIV, Mero and Sable's problems became unbearable. Mero was too jealous, and Sable was too much of a star. On May 31, 1998, Mero beat Sable in a match that meant Sable would have to leave the World Wrestling Federation forever.

But WWF head Vince McMahon became Sable's next knight in shining armor, at least for a while. He reinstated Sable, although he wasn't too happy when Sable showed up for a bikini contest against Jacquelyn wearing a painted-on bathing suit.

Yet there's much more to Sable than just a great body and a beautiful face, as she proved with her victory over Jacquelyn. She blends beauty with genuine athletic ability, and her popularity is growing by leaps and bounds.

What a woman!

Sexy, sultry Sable is more than a spectacularly curvaceous body: this WWF women's champion knows how to wrestle, too!

VITAL STATS

HEIGHT/WEIGHT
5'6", and that's all she's revealing!

BIRTH DATE
August 8, 1967

PRO DEBUT
1996

CHAMPIONSHIP GOLD
One WWF women's championship.

WATCH OUT FOR
The intense look that appears on her beautiful face whenever she's about to execute her "Sable bomb" finisher. Sable might look innocent, but she isn't.

MAXIMUM MADNESS
Just a pretty face? No way! At SummerSlam '98, Sable was out for revenge when she teamed with Edge against Marc Mero and Jacquelyn. She won the match not by pinning Jacquelyn, but by using the TKO—Mero's move—to pin her former mate!

Sabu

Maniacal. Homicidal. Suicidal. Genocidal. All excellent descriptions of Sabu, a wildman whose style is truly incredible.

What is most incredible, though, is that Sabu's astonishingly self-destructive ring style hasn't permanently crippled him by now. When fans go to see Sabu wrestle, they know that they're not going to see professional versions of complex amateur moves and maneuvers. They know they're not going to see honorable displays of sportsmanship and fair play.

They are, however, going to see one of the wildest individuals ever to step—or fly— through the ropes. His singular goal: obliterate his opponent at any and all costs.

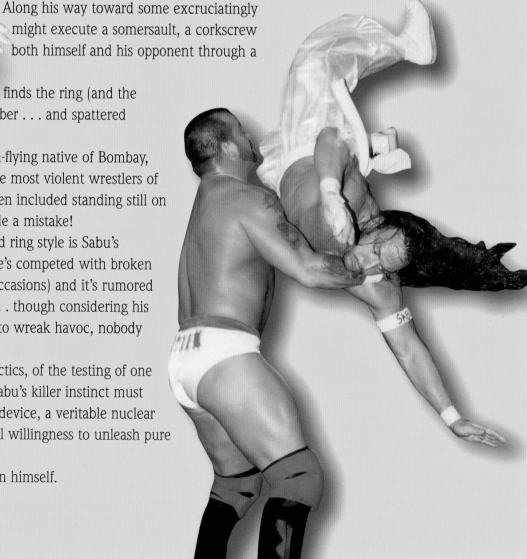

Even when Sabu isn't hurling his body through the air, his face clearly shows the maniacal intensity of his suicidal ring style.

When Sabu isn't hurling his body recklessly around the ring, he's propelling it out of the ring. Along his way toward some excruciatingly painful impact with his foe, Sabu might execute a somersault, a corkscrew twist, or a backwards flip—often crashing both himself and his opponent through a ringside table in the process!

Indeed, the end of a Sabu match usually finds the ring (and the area surrounding the ring) littered with lumber . . . and spattered with lots of blood.

It's no wonder Sabu is so wild. This high-flying native of Bombay, India, was a protege of The Sheik, one of the most violent wrestlers of the '60s and '70s. Part of his training regimen included standing still on hot coals for two minutes each time he made a mistake!

Almost as much of a signature as his wild ring style is Sabu's willingness and ability to wrestle injured. He's competed with broken ribs and a broken cheekbone (on separate occasions) and it's rumored that he often competes with a concussion . . . though considering his inability to speak English and his eagerness to wreak havoc, nobody has every really been able to tell for sure.

If wrestling is a sport of strategies and tactics, of the testing of one man's physical weapons against another's, Sabu's killer instinct must be considered to be the ultimate doomsday device, a veritable nuclear warhead comprised of the explosively primal willingness to unleash pure and absolute violence.

Even . . . and sometimes especially . . . on himself.

Perry Saturn

For years people asked this question: What would happen if Perry Saturn went out on his own? It's no wonder people questioned Saturn's ability to make it as a singles wrestler. After all, although he made his pro debut in 1989, he never achieved much success until he formed The Eliminators with John Kronus in ECW.

Perry Saturn brought his unique brand of extreme intensity from ECW to WCW.

Kronus and Saturn were an outstanding duo, known for their violent approach to tag team wrestling. In the mid-1990s, The Eliminators were the dominant tag team in ECW and one of the best in the world.

The Eliminators had a great 1996. They won the ECW tag team title from Cactus Jack and Mikey Whipwreck on February 3, 1996, and held the belts for six months, an unusually long span in the volatile world of ECW. They lost the belts to arch rivals The Gangstas in August 1996, and regained them four months later. And, after losing the belts again, they came back on April 13, 1997, to beat Buh-Buh Ray and D-Von Dudley for the title. Not a bad feat, considering The Dudleys have since won four more ECW tag titles!

Saturn nearly saw his career end when he landed on an errant crutch and suffered a torn anterior cruciate ligament. He underwent six months of painful rehabilitation and still wasn't 100 percent when he joined WCW in late 1997. But Saturn, a courageous competitor, proved he was ready by beating Disco Inferno for the WCW TV title on November 3, 1997. He lost the belt back to Disco thirty-five days later, and spent most of the next year acting as a virtual bodyguard for Raven.

Now that Raven's Flock has disbanded, good things might start to happen for this unusual, enigmatic, multi-faceted wrestler from Cleveland, Ohio. He has proven numerous times that he can go hold for hold with any wrestler in the world. Sure, he looked stupid when he lost a match to Chris Jericho at the Souled Out '99 pay-per-view and, as a result, had to wear a dress for ninety days. But even while wearing the dress, he won a dog collar match against Jericho at the Uncensored '99 pay-per-view!

Despite his battered knees and ankles, Saturn forges ahead in wrestling. Given his remarkable determination, it's likely that his best championship days are still ahead.

VITAL STATS

HEIGHT/WEIGHT
5'10", 234 lbs.

BIRTH DATE
unknown

PRO DEBUT
1989

CHAMPIONSHIP GOLD
One WCW TV title; three ECW tag team titles.

WATCH OUT FOR
A spectacular splash from the top rope, followed by the "Rings of Saturn," one of the most feared finishing moves in the sport.

MAXIMUM MADNESS
In May 1997, Saturn was involved in a melee with D-Von Dudley and Buh-Buh Ray Dudley when he landed on a crutch thrown by New Jack of The Gangstas. Saturn suffered torn ACL and meniscus ligaments, but returned to the ring six months later.

"Macho Man" Randy Savage

"Macho Man" Randy Savage has paid his dues, both in and out of the ring.

He first broke into the sport in 1973, but it took him more than a decade of competing in various regional promotions before he received his big break. That break came in 1985, when he signed with the World Wrestling Federation. A bidding war among WWF managers ensued for the "Macho Man's" services. The surprise winner: Elizabeth, who had previously been unknown to WWF fans.

Also unknown to WWF fans was the fact that in 1985, Savage and Elizabeth were newlyweds. Perhaps it was their love that helped fuel their ring chemistry; in any event, they met with enormous success in the WWF. He was the brawn, she was the brains. Together they were second only to Hulk Hogan in terms of ruling the federation between 1985 and 1991, the year Savage and Elizabeth were publicly married, at the August 26 Summerslam pay-per-view event.

The following year, Savage and Elizabeth were publicly divorced. The beauty brought out the beast in the "Macho Man." When they were together, his jealousy led to violent feuds with George "The Animal" Steele and Hulk Hogan. When their marriage was crumbling, he took his frustrations out on "Nature Boy" Ric Flair to capture his second WWF World title.

In December 1994, Savage followed Hulk Hogan into the WWF's biggest rival promotion, World Championship Wrestling. During his WCW tenure, Savage has won fifty percent more World titles, but he's also suffered a serious injury: a torn anterior cruciate ligament that has cast serious doubts on his future in the sport.

Yet the injury doesn't seem to seriously bother the "Macho Man," who continues to feud with his ex-wife Elizabeth and his ex-partner Hogan. If the history of Randy Savage's career has taught us anything, it has shown that just when you count the "Macho Man" down and out, he comes back to prove you wrong.

"Oooooh, yeahhhhh!"

"Macho Man" Randy Savage may not display many unique moves in the ring, but personality-wise, he's one of a kind!

VITAL STATS

HEIGHT/WEIGHT
6'2", 237 lbs.

BIRTH DATE
November 15, 1952

PRO DEBUT
1973

CHAMPIONSHIP GOLD
Two WWF World heavyweight titles; one WWF Intercontinental heavyweight title; three WCW World heavyweight titles.

WATCH OUT FOR
The flying elbow delivered with decisive authority as the "Macho Man" launches his body from the second or top turnbuckle.

MAXIMUM MADNESS
In 1989, Savage accused his Megapowers tag team partner, Hulk Hogan, of "lusting after Elizabeth." The result was one of the most violent feuds of the "Macho Man's" career.

Scott Steiner

What kind of man would not only turn against his own brother, but sacrifice the World Championship Wrestling World tag team title in the process? What kind of man would join the New World Order and have no problem targeting his brother for destruction? What kind of man would make so many obscene gestures that he has had to be reprimanded several times by WCW officials?

Scott Steiner, that's who. Between 1998 and 1999, he went from being one of the most popular men in the sport to one of the most hated and controversial.

It was at the SuperBrawl '98 pay-per-view event when "Big Poppa Pump," as he is now known, gave up his brother and the WCW tag belts. A few minutes into Rick and Scott Steiner's World tag team title defense against Scott Hall and Kevin Nash, Scott stood in the center of the ring as Rick crawled under his legs to strike the Steiners' most familiar pose. Instead, Scott smashed his brother in the back.

That devious act marred a career that had seen Scott Steiner establish himself as one of the toughest men in the world, and the Steiner brothers as one of the greatest tag teams of all time. The history of the Steiners in wrestling went back to their amateur days, when Scott and Rick wrestled at the University of Michigan. Rick turned pro in 1983, Scott arrived on the scene three years later, and it didn't take them long to realize they were better off as a team.

Combining power and precision, Rick and Scott rose to the top of the sport, and won three WCW World tag team titles before jumping to the WWF in 1993. Their popularity grew by leaps and bounds, as did their dominance over other tag teams. In the WWF, they won two World tag team titles.

Although both men were hindered by injuries over the next five years, they remained loyal to each other while wrestling in the United States and Japan. Rick and Scott won four more WCW World tag team titles before reaching their bitter end at SuperBrawl.

The man with the Herculean physique and bleach-blond hair has become a key member of the NWO. Scott has fallen in love with the microphone, which he uses to brag about his inside-the-ring and outside-the-ring accomplishments. Too bad loyalty to his brother is something Scott can't brag about.

VITAL STATS

HEIGHT/WEIGHT
6'1", 235 lbs.

BIRTH DATE
July 29, 1962

PRO DEBUT
1986

CHAMPIONSHIP GOLD
Two WWF World tag team titles; six WCW World tag team titles; one WCW TV title.

WATCH OUT FOR
A whip off the ropes, which can be followed by one of Steiner's favorite finishers: his famed Frankensteiner, or the "Steiner recliner." Either way, the match is history!

MAXIMUM MADNESS
The Steiners were already considered one of the top tag teams in the world in 1989, but could they back up that standing by winning the WCW World tag team title? Indeed they could, by beating Michael Hayes and Jim Garvin on November 1, 1989!

Scott Steiner's undergone quite a transformation from the smiling fan favorite to the bleached-blond (and despised) "Big Poppa Pump."

Sting

Sting had already been wrestling for a few years when his March 27, 1988 match with NWA World champion Ric Flair was aired nationally on TBS's "Clash of the Champions." Up until then, he was one of many wrestlers in the sport seeking to break through into the upper echelons.

The next day, after taking the legendary "Nature Boy" to a forty-five-minute draw, Sting was the most talked-about star in the wrestling world!

With a powerful physique and youthful exuberance, as well as visually arresting face paint and charisma to spare, Sting hopped aboard the momentum of his "Clash of the Champions" victory and never looked back!

Ironically, it would be Flair that Sting would defeat—on July 7, 1990—to capture his first major singles title, the NWA World heavyweight championship. His reign was impressive, lasting until Flair upended him on January 11, 1991.

Sting's winning ways have been impressive. In addition to the world titles listed here, the "Stinger" has also captured the WCW U.S. and television titles.

Sting's "scorpion deathlock" is one of the most effective finishing maneuvers that wrestling has ever known.

Since that first big championship win, it seems as if a title belt simply belongs around his waist. When he's wrestling, that is.

Shortly after the renegade NWO was formed in WCW in mid-1996, Sting pulled himself out of active competition. Some saw it as an expression of fear; others saw it as a form of protest. Either way, Sting remained out of the ring for nearly eighteen months, but he never strayed far. Usually, Sting could be spotted up in the rafters of the arena, silently watching the events below.

He finally returned to action, initially as a member of the Wolfpac, a splinter faction within the NWO. But after all these years in the sport and all his success, Sting is not the type to join forces with anyone. He's his own man chasing his own dreams and ideals, and he prefers it that way.

"Owwwwwww!"

VITAL STATS

HEIGHT/WEIGHT
6'2", 260 lbs.

BIRTH DATE
March 20, 1959

PRO DEBUT
1985

CHAMPIONSHIP GOLD
One NWA World heavyweight title; four WCW World heavyweight titles; two WCW World tag team titles.

WATCH OUT FOR
The "Stinger" splash, a hard clothesline delivered when an opponent is backed helplessly into the corner, and the "scorpion deathlock" leglock!

MAXIMUM MADNESS
On March 16, 1997, after keeping the wrestling world guessing for months about which side he would join, Sting answered the doubts loud and clear by attacking his NWO "partners" at WCW's "Uncensored" pay-per-view event and joining the NWO Wolfpac!

VITAL STATS

HEIGHT/WEIGHT
5'11", 221 lbs.

BIRTH DATE
October 11, 1967

PRO DEBUT
1987

CHAMPIONSHIP GOLD
Two ECW tag team titles; two ECW TV titles; one ECW heavyweight title.

WATCH OUT FOR
One of many suplexes, followed by a whip into a propped-up table followed by the "Taz-mission," his favorite finisher.

MAXIMUM MADNESS
Taz wasn't happy when he lost the ECW TV title to Bam Bam Bigelow on March 1, 1998, but the loss enabled him to go on to achieve his championship dream by beating Shane Douglas for the ECW heavyweight title.

TAZ

Some people call him "The Human Suplex Machine." Others say that, pound for pound, Taz is the greatest wrestler in the world.

At first glance, there's nothing special about Taz. He's 5'11", 221 pounds of muscle on a stout, sturdy body that's topped with a round, ferocious-looking face. His eyes are small and intense. A goatee surrounds his firm mouth. His hair is cropped close.

But when Taz vaults into action, watch out!

Over the past two years, Taz has proven to be nearly unbeatable. In fact, Taz grabs headlines whenever he does lose. On June 7, 1997, at the ECW Arena in Philadelphia, Taz defeated Shane Douglas for the ECW TV title. He held the belt for nearly nine months. While champions often lose their matches through disqualification, but retain their belts because they weren't pinned or didn't submit, Taz didn't lose a single match! He steamrolled over the toughest competition ECW could offer.

Even his eventual loss of the title to Bam Bam Bigelow was controversial. Taz caught Bigelow in his "Taz-mission" finisher and just about everybody, except the referee, saw Bigelow tap out, indicating that he wanted to submit. But Bigelow finally escaped the hold by launching himself off the turnbuckle and splashing Taz—right through the ring! Bigelow emerged from the hole with Taz and pinned him.

Never one to be denied, Taz moved on to bigger and better things and pinned Shane Douglas for the ECW heavyweight title on January 10, 1999. "Douglas and I both knew he would never survive a match with me, brother," Taz said after the match. "He ran for a long time, but time runs out on everyone, including Shane Douglas."

Time is certainly not running out for the man who was born Peter Senerchia in Red Hook, New York. After making his pro debut in 1987, Taz spent a long time trying to find a place to catch on, and finally found that his extreme style was perfect for ECW. He formed an outstanding tag team with Kevin Sullivan and they won the ECW tag team title on December 4, 1993. Two years later, Taz and Sabu teamed to win another ECW tag title. But the Taz-Sabu partnership came to a violent end when Bill Alfonso, Sabu's manager, attacked Taz.

The feud between Sabu and Taz has been one of the most fascinating and exciting in all of wrestling. At ECW's Living Dangerously pay-per-view on March 21, 1999, Taz defeated Sabu in a spectacularly brutal match. Afterward, they shook hands.

Intense, violent, and focused, Taz truly is one of the most explosively exciting stars in the sport.

"The Human Suplex Machine" takes down yet another victim!

The Undertaker

Ask not for whom the bell tolls, it tolls for thee . . . at least when The Undertaker is in the building. When the arena house lights darken and The Undertaker takes his long, slow, haunting walk to the ring, every person in the building—and especially the man standing in the ring as his opponent—is wondering the same thing: "Who is this man and where did he come from?"

In reality, his name is Mark Calloway, and he was born in Dallas, Texas. He played college basketball before deciding to become a pro wrestler. Back in his early pro years (1989–1990), he was known as The Master of Pain, Texas Red, and The Punisher. When he arrived in the WCW in 1990 and joined The Skyscrapers, he was known as "Mean" Mark Callous.

But his career didn't really take off until 1991, when he entered the WWF, changed his name to The Undertaker, and set his sights on World champion Hulk Hogan.

Since then, The Undertaker has been one of the most dominant wrestlers in the world. His "tombstone" piledriver is the most awesome finishing maneuver in the sport. He has proven himself immune to punishment, immune to change, even immune to disaster. At the 1998 Royal Rumble, Kane, his alleged half-brother, locked him in a casket and set the whole thing on fire. Somehow, The Undertaker survived.

Survival is what The Undertaker is all about. Even after winning and losing the WWF World title within a six-day span in late 1991, The Undertaker continued his tour of destruction in the WWF, and became one of the most appreciated fan favorites in the federation. Sometimes he got caught up in feuds that, on the surface, seemed to be a waste of his time, but nobody was asking any questions at WrestleMania XIII when he beat Sid Vicious for his second WWF World title.

The past few years have been filled with controversy for The Undertaker. He broke up with manager Paul Bearer, feuded with Kane, nearly won the World title again from "Stone Cold" Steve Austin, made up with Kane, feuded with Kane, reunited with Bearer, and went up against Vince McMahon's Corporation.

But one thing hasn't changed: When the house lights dim and the bell tolls, The Undertaker is a force to be reckoned with.

As mysterious as he is dangerous, The Undertaker's embrace of the "dark side" of life has made him spectacularly popular in the WWF.

VITAL STATS

HEIGHT/WEIGHT
6'9", 328 lbs.

BIRTH DATE
March 24, 1962

PRO DEBUT
1989

CHAMPIONSHIP GOLD
Two WWF World titles.

WATCH OUT FOR
A hard clothesline, which is almost always followed by the "tombstone" piledriver and, inevitably, a three-count.

MAXIMUM MADNESS
Hulk Hogan had held the WWF World title for over eight months when he stepped into the ring against The Undertaker at the 1991 Survivor Series. But he walked out of the ring without the belt, thanks to the combined efforts of the interfering Ric Flair and manager Paul Bearer.

Rob Van Dam

He calls himself "Mr. Monday Night," but ECW standout Rob Van Dam is outstanding on *any* night of the week. This 28-year-old ring tactician is not only one of the finest wrestlers in the world, he's also one of the most controversial. And one of the luckiest, too. Van Dam should have lost the ECW TV title to Jerry Lynn at the Living Dangerously pay-per-view on March 21, 1999, because the referee was ready to hand the belt to Lynn after the 20-minute time limit expired. But Lynn demanded five more minutes so that he could pin Van Dam, and paid the price for his confidence. Within two minutes, Van Dam—with the help of ever-present manager Bill Alfonso—pinned Lynn to retain the title.

Van Dam could be accused of being opportunistic. A few years ago, both the WWF and WCW were bidding for his services. He was seen on both the WWF's "Monday Night Raw" and WCW's "Monday Nitro" broadcasts, so he started calling himself "Mr. Monday Night." The nickname stuck—although many of his most important victories have occurred on Saturday nights at the ECW Arena!

Although he is small by wrestling standards, Van Dam is one of the most versatile wrestlers in the world. He's strong and agile, and his sensational split-legged moonsault and "Van Daminator" finisher are awe-inspiring moves.

This native of Battle Creek, Michigan, was a kick boxer in high school and didn't get involved in professional wrestling until 1989, when he met the original Sheik. Robert Szatowski became Rob Van Dam and the rest, as they say, is history.

Van Dam has been a globetrotter, spanning the world to wrestle in just about every federation there is. He had a celebrated feud with Sabu, during which he claimed to have "destroyed the legend of Sabu." Said Van Dam: "I beat him up so bad that he asked ECW promoters never to sign me against him again." Sabu and Van Dam wrestled each other several more times, but, ironically, they were better as a team. On June 27, 1998, Sabu and Van Dam beat Chris Candido and Lance Storm for their first ECW tag team title.

Van Dam's talents are not limited to the squared circle. He has appeared in two martial arts movies, *Super Fights* and *Blood Moon*. He is also trying to establish a world weightlifting record, which he calls the Van Dam Lift.

Rob Van Dam's unique ring style blends cutting-edge martial arts . . .

. . . with time-tested methods of rulebreaking and brawling.

VITAL STATS

HEIGHT/WEIGHT
6', 237 lbs.

BIRTH DATE
December 18, 1971

PRO DEBUT
1991

CHAMPIONSHIP GOLD
Two ECW tag team titles; one ECW TV title.

WATCH OUT FOR
The chair that Bill Alfonso has just thrown into the ring: Van Dam's "Van Daminator" finisher can't be far behind!

MAXIMUM MADNESS
In 1997, Van Dam wrestled on the WWF's "Monday Night Raw" and WCW's "Monday Nitro" programs, and gave himself the nickname "Mr. Monday Night."

Governor Jesse Ventura

"We shocked the world!"

Indeed, CNN news anchors were literally laughing when they announced that Jesse Ventura had been elected Governor of Minnesota. An ex-pro wrestler? What could the people have been thinking?!

Maybe the people of Minnesota knew something about the man born James Janos that CNN news anchors didn't. Maybe that Ventura is a man of courage and determination.

Before entering pro wrestling, Ventura was a member of the Navy SEALs, an elite corps of underwater demolition experts. Becoming a SEAL required an extensive twenty-two-week training program. "I was in the best physical condition of my life," Ventura said.

After his honorable discharge from the Navy in 1973, Ventura discovered bodybuilding, rode with an outlaw motorcycle club, and attended college.

In 1975 he decided to try pro wrestling. "Surfer" Jesse Ventura made his debut in Kansas City, and soon competed in Oregon and Hawaii. But it wasn't until Jesse "The Body" Ventura began wrestling in the American Wrestling Association in 1979 that the wrestling world began to really take notice.

Two years later, Jesse arrived in the World Wrestling Federation, then returned to the AWA, where he first wrestled Hulk Hogan—on Christmas night, 1982. He would face Hogan again, in 1994, in the WWF. But Jesse's World title hopes were dashed in September 1984, when it was discovered that he had blood clots in his lung.

"The Body" hung up his feather boa and picked up the microphone, and became one of the most popular broadcasters the WWF has ever known. He rode his popularity right to Hollywood, where he appeared in such films as *The Predator* and *The Running Man*.

In 1991, Jesse was elected mayor of Brooklyn Park, Minnesota's sixth-largest city. He served until 1995, and subsequently went into radio broadcasting before scoring his incredible upset for the office of Minnesota governor.

Today, "The Body" wants to be known as "The Mind." Appropriate, because Jesse is the kind of man who succeeds spectacularly at anything to which he puts his mind!

Now that Jesse "The Body" Ventura has been elected governor of Minnesota, he wants to be known as Jesse "The Mind" Ventura.

Celebrity Madness

When the WWF capitalized on the surging popularity of pro wrestling to present the first WrestleMania card on March 31, 1985, it became an event far bigger than the sport itself. Hulk Hogan and Mr. T, tag team partners in the main event, hosted "Saturday Night Live" and appeared on talk shows nationwide.

Just as the wrestlers were becoming celebrities, the spotlight of national attention created by WrestleMania drew celebrities into its lure: New York Yankees ex-manager Billy Martin was a guest ring announcer, world-famous pianist Liberace was a guest timekeeper, pop star Cyndi Lauper was a guest manager, and Muhammad Ali was a special referee.

Since then, WrestleMania has been a major celebrity lure, attracting such stars as Joan Rivers (WrestleMania II ring announcer), Ray Charles (WrestleMania II National Anthem vocalist), Vanna White (WrestleMania IV timekeeper), Alex Trebek (WrestleMania VII ring announcer), Pamela Anderson(WrestleMania XI ring second to Diesel), Jenny McCarthy (WrestleMania XI ring second to Shawn Michaels), and dozens more.

"Stone Cold" Steve Austin has so much attitude, he's not about to back down from anyone . . . not even "Iron" Mike Tyson!

But not all the celebrities of WrestleMania have been merely window dressing.

At WrestleMania II, football stars Jimbo Covert, Bill Fralic, Russ Francis, Ernie Holmes, Harvey Martin, and "Refrigerator" Perry participated in a special invitational battle royal.

At WrestleMania XI, Lawrence Taylor, former football star of the Super Bowl-champion New York Giants, battled — and defeated! — Bam Bam Bigelow. Top 40 rap stars Salt N' Pepa served as LT's ring attendants for the bout.

At WrestleMania XIV, boxing legend Mike Tyson became a troubleshooting referee who caused trouble of his own when he joined the rulebreaking cooperative DeGeneration X. The surprise came when Tyson defected from DX and counted the pin on Shawn Michaels that made "Stone Cold" Steve Austin WWF World champion!

Of course, WrestleMania doesn't have a monopoly on celebrity involvement in wrestling, and didn't pave very much new ground in featuring non-wrestlers on its cards. Legendary boxer Muhammad Ali crossed over into pro wrestling several times, most notably in battling Japanese legend Antonio Inoki to a forgettable 15-round draw in 1976.

Most recently, NBA superstar Dennis Rodman joined forces with NWO leader "Hollywood" Hulk Hogan to battle "Diamond" Dallas Page and the NBA's Karl Malone at WCW's Bash at the Beach pay-per-view event in July 1998. A month later, at WCW's Road Wild pay-per-view card, Hogan teamed with WCW Executive Vice President Eric Bischoff to battle Page and "Tonight Show" host Jay Leno, who was seconded by his multi-talented bandleader, Kevin Eubanks.

Rest assured that as long as the mat sport remains popular, celebrities from other sports and the world of entertainment will be trying their best to get their own firsthand taste of wrestling madness!

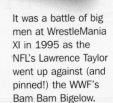

It was a battle of big men at WrestleMania XI in 1995 as the NFL's Lawrence Taylor went up against (and pinned!) the WWF's Bam Bam Bigelow.

NBA superstar Dennis Rodman goes airborne against Lex Luger as The Giant looks on during this 1997 pay-per-view match.

A Brief Chronology of Modern Wrestling Madness

September 17, 1981 · · · · · "Nature Boy" Ric Flair defeats "American Dream" Dusty Rhodes in Kansas City, Missouri, to capture his first NWA World heavyweight title. Flair would go on to capture a total of nine NWA titles, four WCW World titles, and two WWF World titles, through the end of 1998.

January 23, 1984 · · · · · Hulk Hogan defeats The Iron Sheik in New York's Madison Square Garden, signaling the beginning of "Hulkamania."

July 23, 1984 · · · · · Wendi Richter captures the WWF World women's title from The Fabulous Moolah in New York, ending the sport's longest continuous title reign — Moolah had held the belt since defeating Judy Grable in Baltimore on September 18, 1956.

March 31, 1985 · · · · · The WWF's first WrestleMania card is held, at Madison Square Garden in New York City. In the main event, Hulk Hogan and Mr. T defeat Roddy Piper and Paul Orndorff.

November 7, 1985 · · · · · The WWF holds wrestling's first-ever pay-per-view card: The Wrestling Classic, at the Rosemont Horizon in Rosemont, Illinois.

April 25, 1992 · · · · · Jimmy Snuka defeats Wildman Bellomo in Philadelphia to become the first ECW heavyweight champion.

April 29, 1995 · · · · · The largest crowd in wrestling history — an estimated 190,000 people in Mayday Stadium in Pyongyang, North Korea — witnesses Antonio Inoki defeat Ric Flair in the first-ever match between the two mat legends.

July 7, 1996 · · · · · The renegade New World Order is officially christened in WCW as "Hollywood" Hogan joins forces with Scott Hall and Kevin Nash.

July 6, 1998 · · · · · Bill Goldberg defeats "Hollywood" Hogan in Atlanta, Georgia, to capture the WCW World heavyweight title.

November 3, 1998 · · · · · Jesse "The Body" Ventura — who now wants to be known as Jesse "The Mind" Ventura — is elected Governor of Minnesota.